Poems from a Restless Traveler

Terry Loncaric

ISBN: 978-81-19654-48-2

First Edition: 2024
Rs. 200/-

Cyberwit.net
HIG 45 Kaushambi Kunj, Kalindipuram
Allahabad - 211011 (U.P.) India
http://www.cyberwit.net
Tel: +(91) 9415091004
E-mail: info@cyberwit.net

Printed at Repro India Limited.

Devoted to Debbie, my best traveling companion in life and on vacation adventures.

Contents

Restless Ramblings

The Seeker

If I had not traveled,
I would not have grasped
the sun-drenched immensity
of the Golden Gate bridge
on a slow moving boat.
I would have missed
the tart ocean air,
the slap of rhythmic waves,
on a horseback ride in Jamaica.
If I wasn't adventurous,
I would have missed
the bargaining frenzy
of the friendly, chaotic,
crazy flea market in Cancun.
I would not have taken
a ski lift to a mountaintop
in Lake Tahoe to admire
nature's miracle,
the emerald green
reflections of pine trees
on a shimmering lake.
The seeker in me
keeps free-falling,
enjoying every morsel
of my travel experiences.
I only know one truth,
to travel where
my soul leads me.

World Travelers

My niece Angie speaks fluent Mandarin,
she ate bugs in China on a dare,
she loved the depth of the
Chinese landscape from the
plunging Great Wall.
My friend Susan conquered the lush
Highlands of Scotland before
whirling madly in a bar
with a charming man named Angus
on the romantic island of Skye.
Ex co-worker Suzanne
rowed the canals of Venice
with her daughter Jackie, watching
images of weathered buildings
as they slowly flickered in the water.
They relaxed in a neighborhood cafe,
bursting with laughter as they
struggled to emulate the musical
rhythms of the Italian language.
Some days I bask in the stories
of traveling far and wide,
glimpses of the globe shared
in the post card memories
of my adventurous
family and friends.

New Orleans Quintet

My Siren

You are my siren,
the first place I visited
to escape the tearing,
twisting knife of grief.
I needed your noise,
embraced your craziness,
drenched myself
in your kaleidoscope
of pulsing colors,
your Southern
eccentricities,
your amplified characters.
Of course, I found
the photograph
of Tennessee Williams
in the hotel lobby
when I was looking
for a bathroom,
immediately discovering
there are no accidents
in New Orleans.
Stealer of my soul,
your music heals me,
your saints and sinners
comfort me.
Even when I think
I am finished with you,
I take in your grittiness,
gasp at your grandeur,

blinded, burned-out.
banged up by life,
New Orleans,
I still need you
to remind me
I am alive.

Morning in the French Quarter

No naughty neon,
just a fried-egg-of-a-rising sun,
the stillness that drizzles
a city ravaged by noise
the night before.
A requiem of delivery trucks
leans against the steam.
Blossoms waft.
Cathedral bells awaken.
A Southern breeze trembles.
One last chance to feel the
presence of God
in a sunrise that lights the dome
of the St. Louis Cathedral on fire.

This Elf/This Alley Cat

Three times
in less than four days
I keep bumping
into the tarot reader
in New Orleans
with the cowboy hat,
a sign I should have
my cards read.
I love his spirit.
This self-proclaimed
cowboy from Canada
tells me I am an elf,
my mother was an elf,
we bore easily,
seek adventure.
So I roam the streets
of New Orleans,
eat spicy food,
something I rarely do.
I admire the Spanish moss
that drips from
gigantic oak trees
in this most exotic
of Southern cities.
I observe a cool
jazz drummer
flip his sticks
in mid-air,
and never lose

the rhythm of
his mischievous beat.
I watch three
adolescent rats
in a courtyard
fight for crumbs
of a beignet
without freaking out.
I catch the chaos,
absorb the energy of
my surroundings,
occasionally retreat
into the sacred silence.
A lazy observer.
A prowling alley cat.
I am cool.
I am crazy.
I am free.

She Had Flowers in Her Hair

A block from Bourbon Street
on a relatively quiet
street corner, she stood out.
A young folk singer,
dark hair, penetrating gaze,
relaxed vibe.
Does Joni Mitchell have
a granddaughter?
She sang folk songs
about love and heart-ache,
about life and struggle.
She reminded me
of my college days,
when young people
congregated in a meadow
before classes began.
Someone always had
a guitar, shared a riff,
sang a song.
I felt young again,
watching a woman
in a loose-fitting dress
with flowers in her hair.
She swayed and sang,
her voice drenching
my happy ears, my tired soul.
The light changed.
I stayed for a few more tunes,
blurted out,
"You have the voice of an angel."
She smiled, kept singing.

New Orleans Mist

A glow on the streets
rolls in the morning mist.
All of the buildings,
even the trickles of rain.
melt into a softness.
The blurry images
reel me in.

Other Gems

Effervescent Savannah

In this grand Southern city,
I could feel the ghosts
of artists, drag queens,
and literary icons
indulge me with
their rambling stories,
tinged with history
and their genteel
Southern upbringing.
Even the drunken
tour guide
stumbling off
the bus charmed me.
His scraped face looked
like he had been in a
barroom brawl
the night before.
Like a tango that
makes the blood
rush to my head,
I feel the effervescence
of Savannah:
its lush gardens,
its quaint courtyards,
and its wild waterfront
life.

Oh, Sedona

Your rugged rocks
bleed red, gold, and orange,
drenched with age
and the miracle of geology.
Your prickly pears
dance with dainty
purple wildflowers that
create a silhouette when
they catch the glint of the sun.
Elegant ravines and
lush pine forests reveal
breathtaking views along
narrow, winding roads.
Mountain ranges spill layers
of copper brown and misty blue
that melt into the colors of the horizon.
Arizona, you were not the craggy
old man desert-scape I was expecting.
Your mixture of vibrant colors
and shapes wrangled my senses,
spoke my prayers
with loud majesty, and yes,
with quiet certainty.

Peaceful Portland

Searching in the old
historic neighborhood
of Portland, Maine
for a steaming bowl
of chowder,
felt sidetracked
while watching a man
leave his car parked
with the motor running,
the car door askew.
He dashed into
a flower shop to collect
a fresh bouquet,
not the least bit surprised
his car was still there.
On streets of cobblestone,
I discovered aromatic
bakeries, intimate galleries,
cool cafes.
However, the memory
of the man and his flowers
lingered.
It felt life-changing
to enjoy cosmopolitan
pleasures in such
a laid-back, quaint
New England town.
Rarely see that level
of trust amid
such unique beauty.

California

California U.S.A.

I do not mind you are
flirty, occasionally shallow.
You wander and roam,
amble and meander
over rocky cliffs.
along sloping farmlands,
past crashing waves.
You expose your flesh,
change the colors
of your wardrobe
in a hot second.
With the precision
of your native bird, the Condor,
you swoop down upon me,
push me to the edge
of your hairpin turns,
your killer inclines,
plunging gently into
your laughing, murky
waves.

On the Wharf

Tables with steaming lobster tails,
dark roasts brewing,
sour dough baking.
Take your pick
of wafting aromas.
Wicked good drummer.
A little boy.
It doesn't matter.
He keeps the beat.
Strolling guitar player
serves mellow riffs.
Oblivious to the noise,
sea lions play and dance.
Much larger animals
than you imagined.
Sights and sounds flicker
fast and furious,
long and drawn-out.
The pace is yours to set.
A ticker tape of
travelers from
every region,
every country,
dressed to kill,
dressed with
the grime of the streets.
The vibe of the water,
the flavor of many lands,
primitive,

yet unapologetically
commercial.
A day to give in
to the beat,
a day to experience
Fisherman's Wharf,
a San Francisco treat.

Golden Gate Park

A meandering path
twisting,
turning,
over bridges,
roaming past
flowers,
manicured bushes,
ancient trees
with endless roots.
An invitation
to slowly unravel
the layers
of the forest,
seek solace
in nature's symmetry.
I keep returning
to the forest's serenity,
to understand
the meaning in shadows,
the intricacies of flowers,
the gentle ripple
of wind on the water.
I keep returning
to the shimmer of colors,
the serene landscapes,
listening to their secrets,
so ancient, so familiar.

The Tropics

Florida Rainbow

After a night
of brewing storms,
after the ocean
simmers, spews,
and exhausts itself,
there is a clarity
of light that breaks
through the morning
horizon, spills upon
the water.
A morning walk
to awaken the soul.
A moment to watch
the clouds crouch
upon gentle waves,
smiling, dancing
into the light.
An arc of a rainbow
paints the horizon,
waits for me
to step inside,
to become lost
in this drenched,
perfect canvas,
to feel
the peacefulness
inside this moment.

Pastel Buildings

Any moment I expect to see
Don Johnson roll up
in his sportscar
wearing his pastel jacket,
the wind whipping
his "Miami Vice" hair.
I love the breezy,
beachy quality of Florida
buildings, a bit sassy,
somewhat dreamy.
A gingerbread house on "acid,"
a sexy "Miami Vice" episode
that never ends.
As I take in a dreamscape
of pastel buildings with
vivid windows and shutters,
I know I will soon
squish my toes
through soft sand,
feel the spray of the ocean,
submerge myself
in a tropical pastiche
of palm trees and pina coladas.
The colors of Florida
are the colors of freedom.

Gulf Coast Meditation

I came for the donuts.
I stayed
for the exotic black birds,
the stillness of the water,
the streaks of a pink horizon,
the absence of people.
I stayed.
I listened
to the gentlest
breath of the wind.
I understood.

Florida Tiki Bar

We sat on high bar stools.
Everything, from the grassy roof
to the torches, felt tropical.
A singer, really a one-man band,
told awful jokes, sang cover tunes.
He fit the cheesy atmosphere.
Even when he appeared
snarky, it was a part of
his lounge lizard act.
A perfect place for
sharing crab legs,
tropical beverages,
flirty glances.
Let's watch the tide
roll in, while we wait
for Jimmy Buffett's ghost.
Two laid-back beach bums.
We have all the time
in the world.

San Juan Disco

A heat wave
of sexiness.
Bodies pressed
on a dance floor,
gyrating, twirling
on splashes of light
that flickered and blinked
to pulsating rhythms.
Heads throbbing.
Bodies aching.
Somehow we had
the stamina back then
to close down
a San Juan disco
and stagger back
to our floating
hotel on the water.
Those were the days!

Bermuda Trance

Pristine and clean.
Wind-blown and sun-dappled.
Even the cab drivers stop
at day's end to admire
the breathtaking view
from the tops of
the grassy cliffs.
The tall grasses sway
against the steady sweep
of the inky blue Atlantic.
A soothing place
to become lost
in the sweet dreams
of an observant beach bum.
I felt drawn to the water,
gently lapping,
then slamming
the perfect pink sand
in dramatic rhythms.
The refined homes
in pastel rows,
the mysterious caves.
the submerged
volcanic rocks
entranced me in
their rugged beauty,
made me stop
with my cab driver

one last time
to watch
the fiery arc
of the sun.

Chicago

Chicago Images

Brawny and beautiful.
The smokestacks
float swirly patterns
above the tall brick factories.
The sharp screech of trains
halting and gasping,
rattling window panes
in an eerie music.
The flamenco rhythms
of pedestrians
clicking and clacking,
leaping almost gracefully
over gaping potholes
as large as small rivers.
The dissonance of
conversations, spiced with
the inflections of many
lands and regions.
A jagged, massive stretch
of skyscrapers
hovering above
a monster lake.
A heap of corruption.
A microcosm of humanity.
Always self-deprecating.
Forever exhausted,
yet never giving up.
Somehow beautiful.

Smiling Virgin Mary

Children chase fruit trucks.
Dogs chase children.
A neighborhood with row houses,
creaky porches, close quarters.
Awakens in dusty sunlight.
Boom boxes compete with
the clang of cathedral bells,
sweet bakery aromas,
the tang of spicy tacos.
If you walk through Chicago's
Pilsen neighborhood,
you see survivors,
people who live on love,
mischief, and prayers.
On the window sills of
cramped dwellings
that shake with the breeze,
there are bright, glowing
Virgin Mary altars all around.
In the amber candlelight,
you can swear Mary is smiling.

Reflections on Washington Island (Wisconsin)

On the Front Porch

So this is where you were courted,
road bikes on a country road
with your dear husband.
On this front porch
of a family farm house,
your husband
brought you steaming coffee.
You shared secrets and intimacies,
in the crisp, rural air
of a tucked-away Wisconsin island.
Now you share strong coffee,
bird songs, secrets of old loves,
possibilities of new loves,
with me, your new friend.
The presence of your man
infiltrates the air, a swath of
flashbacks — bitter and sweet.
Still you welcome me to your
quaint little island, your happy escape,
your oasis of family memories.
Our lives are so different, yet I am
reminded, grief alters everyone of us,
yet we find lasting comfort
in our morning rituals.

A Conversation with Trees

Tracing your shadows.
Listening to your stories.
Following your vibrations.
Noticing your sensual curves.
On a winding country road,
I feel the strong winds whip
through ancient trees
that refuse to break.
I wonder, why do trees embrace
growing old, but we humans
run away from the sweet wisdom
of advanced years?

A Paradise for a Poet

The ferry ride to Washington
Island in Northern Door County
thrashed in its fury.
Perhaps it was destined,
to reach a place so serene,
so primitive, so protected,
you must endure the elements.
I loved its island charms,
the snappy reminders,
from barkeepers and their wait staff,
they have a way of doing things.
The compact nature of
the island breeds familiarity,
intimate discourse with strangers,
a peek into a world
that is exotic in its isolation.
Home to artists, farmers,
fishermen, and wealthy retirees,
who live deep in the forest in
impressive log mansions.
A place of crystal blue waters,
primeval forests, and rugged cliffs.
A merging of lush landscapes
and abundant ecosystems.
Cows with beautiful spotted markings.
Fawns grazing by the roadside.
Turkey vultures settling on rooftops.
A sweep of sandhill cranes too many to count.
A rare enclave of unspoiled nature and lasting roots.
A paradise for a poet.

A Place of Characters

Chatting it up on the porch
of the coffee joint with the locals,
who call themselves "lifers."
On Washington Island, in the far reaches
of Northern Wisconsin, it is easy to do that,
so much to observe in this rural,
quaint, yet vividly artistic terrain.
A place where people love the
history of their homesteads
and thrive on the gossip of the lifers.
A land of quaint curiosities.
A wooded property with dangling
clocks, all stuck at 5 o'clock,
an almost surreal reminder,
time has stopped here.
An abandoned farm-truck
with a brightly painted chicken,
left as a treasured relic of
the island's rural Wisconsin roots.
A homey cafe run by sisters,
who serve their special soups,
sandwiches, and pies with just
a smidge of snappy banter.
There are characters around every bend.
The retired kindergarten teacher
goes everywhere with her labradoodle,
since he has separation anxiety.
Not sure, though, who rescued whom.

The husky shop keeper with the long, white
beard could pass for a Viking,
even though he came from Indiana.
The seemingly shy waitress
from the roadside cafe
delights in sharing her passions
for poetry and astrology.
A place of gentle, quirky souls.
Almost everyone has a back story.

A Wisconsin Hollyhock

Peerless flesh,
large round face,
a single hollyhock
sporting lovely,
bright shades of pink,
standing tall
on a sensual stalk,
drinking sunshine,
finding majesty and grace
in the smallest gust
of wind.

Canada

Riding the Rails

Craggy old man
with stony grace
greets me from
his heavenly perch.
I can see his snowy
overcoat,
his wafting blue smoke,
the steep ascent
of his rugged contours.
A misty rain softens
his appearance
like an impressionistic
painting that saturates
the horizon.
A young woman on a train
chugging slowly
through the Canadian Rockies
remembers the first time
she beheld his ancient beauty
like it was yesterday.

Vancouver, B.C.

Bars with rooftop, mountain views.
Nightclubs with throbbing,
all-night rock'n'roll.
Half nature/half evolving
metropolis with
an exotic atmosphere.
Intense creativity.
Bold graffiti
in bathrooms,
on the sides of buildings.
Gas light on cobblestone.
Old World treasures
anoint your streets.
You are more Euro-chic
than bargain basement trendy.
I fell in love
with your stylish, urban edge.
Where else would a stripper
dance to Lou Reed?
Hey Sugar, take a walk
on the wild side.
A land of delicious beats.
Cerebral cultures.
Welcoming strangers,
who voraciously feed off
the curiosity of others.
They call you the San Francisco
of Western Canada.
I just call you Vancouver, B.C.

The Hot Springs of Banff

It's an odd
combination.
Icicles on hair.
The vapors of
cold breath.
The warm bubbles
of the springs.
A blue-streaked
mountain range
encircling
the horizon.
The liquid gold
of sunshine
dripping through
the mountains.
A healing
moment.

New Mexico

Drive to Taos

A spill of sunlight
from above.
Some people see God's
penetrating gaze.
Georgia O'Keeffe saw
a horizon that could
disappear inside
a swirly, fiery canvas.
In nature's light,
I feel the vastness of my life,
the meandering paths
of hope and restoration,
the steepness
of my imagination,
the strength of
the earth's soothing embrace.
In this silvery stillness,
I am swimming
inside Georgia's gush of colors,
melting into this
perfect moment of grace.

Lightning in the Desert

On this peaceful
drive though the desert
when sunlight chased
streaks of flames
through the clouds
and bathed
stony mountain peaks
in a golden silhouette,
a thunderstorm
scattered
the vivid colors
of my perfect canvas.
A fist of lightning
tore through the clouds
like the boom of a cannon,
split the horizon
into two perfect halves,
etched in a silvery light.
The most magnificent
laser light show of my life.
The temperamental forces
of nature assault, then bedazzle.
Life is similar, so raw,
so fear-inducing, yet beautiful
and breathtaking.

Taos Trail

It was a mountainous terrain.
The trail leader and his hippy wife
led me and my mellow horse
up a rocky path.
They shared a quick hit
of their marijuana.
It made the steep trail
feel less daunting.
Below us a huge drop.
Above us, only sky.
My horse occasionally
stopped, as if he knew
I wanted to linger
in certain places,
absorb open spaces.
A terrain kissed
by perfect light,
aflame with the colors of
sagebrush, dancing
along rich earth.
We rose and dipped
just like the tumbleweed,
a free-fall for the senses.

Delightful Delicacies

Lobster Ecstasy

The deep forest
greens of Maine.
A sapphire horizon
that could open its
mouth and swallow
me in its purity.
The heavy perfume
of native trees.
Seal pups playing
in the frothy waters
of the ocean.
Oldies cranked
high on the radio.
Left home with
a broken heart,
needed the whimsy
of a road adventure.
As I zigged and zagged,
along forests, the
ocean, and quaint
little towns,
I almost missed it —
the humble lobster stand
with its aroma of
succulent, sweet meat
on a huge buttery
roll, wrapped tightly
in paper, like a baby
in a blanket.

No fancy extras,
just the mouth-melting
crustacean.
The best meal
I ever had on a picnic table with strangers.
So good it made me
want to moan out loud.
But the strangers
might not have understood.
Sometimes food induces
such ecstasy, such primal
pleasures, you just have
to stop and shout,
"DAMN!"

A Traveling Foodie

A traveling foodie.
I love to dip and taste,
chew and savor, sniff and devour.
A flaky spinach pie, just a hint
of nutmeg, with chatty friends
in a suburban shopping mall.
A fork-tender steak at a
landmark hotel in Milwaukee,
did I say Milwaukee?
A gourmet corned beef hash
prepared by a Japanese chef
at a casual diner in San Francisco.
Fluffy, fried beignets in a
New Orleans courtyard with
spiked coffee and the waft of jazz.
A stop along the scenic California coast
to hear the crash of the waves,
to enjoy the simple pleasures
of creamy avocado wedges
planted upon the most perfect burger.
A detour here, a meal there,
my taste buds are naughty pleasured.
A foodie's work is never done.

Creatures — Great & Small

The Cats of Jamaica

At a Jamaican resort,
the resident cats roamed free,
mingled with the tourists.
It was obvious they didn't
take "no" for an answer.
I had many favorites,
they all had different
personalities, but most
of the cats were friendly.
I loved the way they circled
and nuzzled close when I
feasted on a hand-made pizza.
They always came back for more,
such beggars, such attention whores.
These cats had great "game,"
they would hang with you
for a while, then move on
to the next tourist.
Their soft rubs, tantalizing purrs
mixed with the sounds of the ocean.
Music to my ears.

Baby Penguins

One look,
was it instant love,
was it infatuation,
or simply, a beguiling moment
spent with animal friends,
even if they are in captivity?
How could I possibly
walk past their rocky confines,
overlook their silly antics,
their beautiful splashes,
their Charlie Chaplin gait,
their stunning,
synchronized movements?
Adorable? You agree.
A moment well spent
with the baby penguins
at the Monterey Bay Aquarium.

The Pelicans of Florida

Immense white birds
that crash the waves
at demon speeds,
scooping the catch
of the day with so much
grace and gusto.
From a cafe window,
we watch pelicans in
rapid succession
slam into the water
and stuff their pouches.
We humans order
the catch of the day
that someone else caught.
Pelicans are so much
more methodical,
they swoop upon
the water with
deadly accuracy,
They swallow mounds of fish.
Then they come back for more.
An all-you-can-eat oceanic buffet.
They teach us what it means
to work for your supper.
They teach us the magnificent
lessons of survival.

Music — Near & Far

Flamenco in Santa Fe

Almost prowled past
the hole-in-the-wall tavern,
hidden on a side street.
The intimate space
alluring in its darkness.
I felt the smoldering heat,
the urgency of their dance,
ripe for seduction.
His eyes shot flames
while his finger flickered
robust guitar chords.
She arched and swayed,
clicked her heels,
billowed her skirt.
Higher and faster.
Faster and higher.
A tidal wave
of clicking castanets
and gasping sighs.
My drink shook
to the edge of the table,
almost shattering,
the tingle of seduction
glistening on my skin.

Recital in Montreal

After a long day of
walking, first in Old Montreal,
then downtown,
I stepped into
a magnificent cathedral,
just to rest my feet,
and enjoy the lovely ambience
of a recital in the sacred glow
of stained glass.
The pianist dove into
his performance,
coaxing storminess, rage,
and passion from each note.
Then he caressed the keys
with such gentleness,
you felt the soft vibrations,
the warmth inside every note.
I cannot remember
the musician's name,
just the feeling of being
enveloped in a magic bubble
of old architecture and music
that was sublime and other-worldly.

Indianapolis Jazz Bar

A cramped, corner stage
in an odd-shaped bar.
Wafting in the blur
of neighborhood regulars,
pin-striped suits, raggedy casuals,
untame conversations.
Jazz musicians lean
into the tight window space
with a languid, familiar grace.
They fondle, press, coax
their instruments,
flaunt the midnight hour,
tease and stretch every
wicked improvisation.
They are wild, wailing,
rhythm-crazed cats,
sultans of swing,
masters of seduction,
pumping our veins full
of warm, pungent jazz
in a cozy place
where music stirs and twitches
lonely souls and hungry bodies.

Chicago Blues Bar

It is the faces I notice
contorted in pain,
twisted in pleasure.
The smoky voices.
The blistering licks
of an electric guitar.
There is nothing
quite as cathartic
as the blues.
Joy, wrapped in pain,
served on a delicious riff.
A bittersweet meditation.
The religion of the people.
The heat of the truth.
How I love to feel
every gritty emotion
of the blues.

If you're looking for that special, joyful place on earth to heal your soul or connect your spirit to God, please read Terry Loncaric's *Poems from a Restless Traveler*. Terry's kaleidoscope of travel poems takes you far beyond a typical travelogue by capturing the spiritual essence of every city, landscape, and roadhouse she encounters. Terry's vibrant imagery paints an alluring picture of every haven from the Taos Trail to the Hot Springs of Banff and reveals their powerful mysteries.

Mary Paleologos
Writer/Editor

In her *Poems from a Restless Traveler*, poet Terry Loncaric takes us along for the ride as she travels around the U.S., Canada, and the Caribbean, sharing with them the joys of her experiences. The poet begins with her New Orleans Quintet, clearly her favorite place to visit. Then she takes us on a trip around the U.S., Canada, and the Caribbean, including a visit home to Chicago and nearby Washington Island in Wisconsin. In each visit, the reader learns something about the people who live there and the uniqueness of each spot. When she's done taking us on her poetic itinerary, Terry brings us back to these locations by sharing with us the regional cuisines that she loves, the animals that are endemic to these places, and the music that draws her back. In addition, she has her own unique commentary, such as in A Conversation with the Trees. "I wonder, why do trees embrace growing old, but we humans run away from the sweet wisdom of advanced years?" Thoughtful and delightful!

Judith MK Kaufman
Editor, East on Central

www.ingramcontent.com/pod-product-compliance
Lightning Source LLC
LaVergne TN
LVHW091228150826
845673LV00003B/1065

* 9 7 8 8 1 1 9 6 5 4 4 8 2 *